T0022323

Published by
Little Genius Books
Livingston, NJ 07039, USA
www.littlegeniusbooks.com

ISBN 978-1-953344-64-9

Distributed by
Simon & Schuster, Inc.
1230 Avenue of the Americas
New York, NY 10020, USA

Copyright © 2022 Bottle Cap Book Publishing Services

All rights reserved. No part of this publication may be reproduced, stored in a retrieval system, or transmitted in any form or by any means (including electronic, mechanical, photocopying, recording, or otherwise) without the prior written permission from the publisher.

Printed in China, April 2022

10 9 8 7 6 5 4 3 2 1

This product conforms to all applicable CPSC and CPSIA standards.

For information about custom editions, special sales and premium and corporate purchases, please contact Little Genius Books at info@littlegeniusbooks.com.

# Grandma's Garden

By
Toni Armier

Illustrated by
Lynn Horrabin

LiTtle
GENIUS
BOOkS

My grandma has a special spot
for lettuce, peas, and apricots.

"Let me show you, little one—
a garden can be lots of fun."

First we pull out
all the weeds.

Those are the plants
that no one needs.

We put the seeds in little holes
and wrap tall beanstalks
around their poles.

"Every plant needs water to grow.

Fill the can and tip just so."

"Be careful—some plants like it dry and get their water from the sky."

Golden marigolds bloom today.
They help keep the bugs away.

Some plants are ready
for us to eat.

The tomatoes are fat,
and the peaches are sweet.

"Make sure you only choose the best—
when we pick fruit it's called a harvest."

In my mouth a berry bursts!
"Honey, be sure to wash them first!"

We take the fruits and veggies in.
Now the cooking can begin!

Tomato soup and fresh peach pie—
I love Grandma's garden,
and this is why!